Courageous Heroes of the American West

John C. Frémont
Courageous Pathfinder
of the Wild West

William R. Sanford and Carl R. Green

Enslow Publishers, Inc.
40 Industrial Road
Box 398
Berkeley Heights, NJ 07922
USA

http://www.enslow.com

Original edition published as *John C. Frémont: Soldier and Pathfinder* in 1996.

Library of Congress Cataloging-in-Publication Data

Sanford, William R. (William Reynolds), 1927–

  John C. Frémont : courageous pathfinder of the Wild West / William R. Sanford
and Carl R. Green.

     p. cm. — (Courageous heroes of the American West)

  Earlier edition has subtitle: Soldier and pathfinder.

  Includes index.

  Summary: "Examines the life of explorer John C. Frémont, including his western
expeditions over the Rocky Mountains, mapping California and Oregon, fighting for
California's independence, his life as a soldier and politician, and his legacy as the
Pathfinder"—Provided by publisher.

  ISBN 978-0-7660-4008-3

  1. Frémont, John Charles, 1813–1890—Juvenile literature. 2. Explorers—United States—
Biography—Juvenile literature. 3. Generals—United States—Biography—Juvenile literature.
4. Presidential candidates—United States—Biography—Juvenile literature. I. Green, Carl R.
II. Title.

  E415.9.F8S25 2013

  978'.02092—dc23

  [B]

                         2011042440

Future editions:

Paperback ISBN 978-1-4644-0091-9

ePUB ISBN 978-1-4645-0998-8

PDF ISBN 978-1-4646-0998-5

032012 Lake Book Manufacturing, Inc., Melrose Park, IL

Printed in the United States of America

10 9 8 7 6 5 4 3 2 1

To Our Readers: We have done our best to make sure all Internet addresses in this book were active
and appropriate when we went to press. However, the author and the Publisher have no control over,
and assume no liability for, the material available on those Internet sites or on other Web sites they
may link to. Any comments or suggestions can be sent by e-mail to comments@enslow.com or to the
address on the back cover.

✪ Enslow Publishers, Inc., is committed to printing our books on recycled paper. The paper in every
book contains 10% to 30% post-consumer waste (PCW). The cover board on the outside of each book
contains 100% PCW. Our goal is to do our part to help young people and the environment too!

Ilustration Credits: Brigham Young University, Harold B. Lee Library, Special Collections, p. 19;
© 2011 Clipart.com, a division of Getty Images, p. 7; Enslow Publishers, Inc., p. 20; © Enslow
Publishers, Inc. / Paul Daly, p. 1; The Granger Collection, NYC, p. 15; Library of Congress Prints and
Photographs, pp. 12, 25, 29, 30, 34, 38, 43; © 2010 by the University of South Florida, p. 40.

Cover Illustration: © Enslow Publishers, Inc. / Paul Daly.

Contents

Authors' Note 4

Chapter 1
The Struggle for California 5

Chapter 2
Finding a Path in Life 9

Chapter 3
Marriage and New Adventures 13

Chapter 4
The Fateful Third Expedition 18

Chapter 5
The Court-Martial 23

Chapter 6
A Near Disaster and a Golden Beginning 27

Chapter 7
The Pathfinder Runs for President 32

Chapter 8
Two Commands, Two Failures 36

Chapter 9
Fortunes Made and Lost 41

Glossary 45

Further Reading
(Books and Internet Addresses) 47

Index 48

Authors' Note

This book tells the true story of John Charles Frémont. During his lifetime, many people knew him by his nickname: the Pathfinder. He was a courageous and determined explorer and a distinguished army officer. The newspapers of the day ran lengthy reports on his adventurous journeys throughout the West. You may doubt that one man could pack so much adventure and achievement into a single lifetime. If so, rest easy. All of the events described in this book are drawn from firsthand reports.

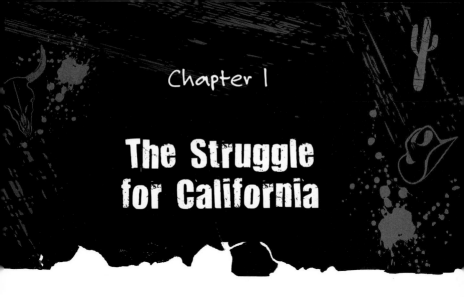

Chapter 1

The Struggle for California

In 1845, the Congress of the United States voted to annex Texas. That act caused friction with Mexico. Should the Texas-Mexico border be set at the Rio Grande, or at the Nueces River? Fighting broke out the following spring. As the war heated up, some American leaders looked farther west. They dreamed of a land that stretched from "sea to shining sea."

Captain John Charles Frémont helped make the dream come true. For years, he had been exploring new routes to the Pacific coast. In early June 1846, he led his mountain men into northern California. His orders were as vague as his purpose was clear. Exploration could wait. California must be free!

Frémont reached California just as events were reaching a climax. Calling themselves Los Osos (The Bears), the American settlers struck the first blow.

Governor José Castro was gathering supplies for his army. On June 10, Los Osos stole 150 of his horses. Before Castro could react, they marched on the town of Sonoma. The Mexican defenders gave up after a brief battle. On June 15, a handmade flag rose over the fort. The flag featured a red star and a brown bear above the words "California Republic."

Frémont set up a command post at Sutter's Fort, near Sacramento. By now, 234 tough, well-armed men had joined him in his quest. When Frémont heard that Castro was planning to retake Sonoma, he marched at once to the settlers' aid. Los Osos welcomed Frémont and made him their commander. News that the United States and Mexico were at war reached California on July 2. With war declared, the U.S. Navy could take a hand.

On July 7, Commodore John Sloat sailed into Monterey Bay. A few days later, the Stars and Stripes also flew over Yerba Buena (today's San Francisco). Even there, Frémont had played a role. Some months before, his raiding party had wrecked the guns at Yerba Buena's Fort Point. Frémont also gave the bay's beautiful entrance its name—the Golden Gate.

The forceful Commodore Robert Stockton replaced Sloat. One of his first acts was to promote Frémont to

John C. Frémont hoists the brown-bear flag as California settlers celebrate their declaration of independence from Mexico. This historic series of events became known as the Bear Flag Revolt.

lieutenant colonel. With the new rank went command of the Naval Battalion of Mounted Volunteer Horsemen. Frémont, an army officer, obeyed the commodore's orders. The country was at war.

Events moved quickly. On July 17, Frémont's unit captured the San Juan Bautista mission. They found some of Castro's supplies hidden there. Two days later, the horsemen rode into San Jose. The next target was San Diego. After a rough sea voyage, the battalion took the city without firing a shot. Castro had fled.

When Los Angeles fell, Frémont thought the war in California was over. On August 31, he marched north.

The Americans, however, had overlooked a very stubborn foe. California's Mexican landowners, the Californios, rose in revolt. The small U.S. force in Los Angeles surrendered to them. In late November, Frémont rode south to face this new threat. Heavy rains slowed his march. On December 27, the battalion limped into Santa Barbara. A few days earlier, Frémont had planned to burn the city. He spared it when the locals promised to end their revolt.

The Californios near Los Angeles were caught in a trap. Frémont was driving south. General Stephen Kearny was marching north from San Diego. The Californios feared Kearny. They knew he would want to avenge his defeat at San Pascual. On balance, it seemed better to surrender to Frémont. On January 13, their leaders met Frémont at Cahuenga Pass.

The Californios agreed to lay down their arms. In return, Frémont promised that the United States would respect their lives and property. The next day, he rode into Los Angeles at the head of his soldiers. The mud-smeared men marched proudly behind their colonel. The soldier-explorer's South Carolina childhood must have seemed long ago and far away.

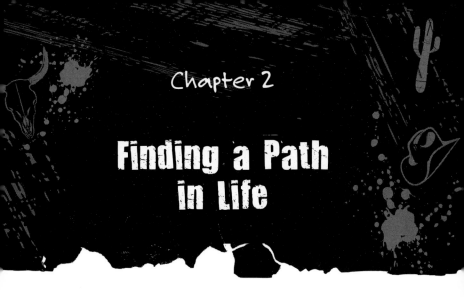

Chapter 2

Finding a Path in Life

John Charles Frémont had his first brush with death in 1814. The one-year-old was sleeping in a Nashville hotel room. Out in the hallway, two men started shooting. A stray bullet smashed through the wall. The slug missed the baby by just inches. A moment later, the duel was over. Andrew Jackson, the future president, lay wounded. The victor was Thomas Hart Benton. In a twist of fate, the grown-up Frémont later married one of Benton's daughters.

The events that led to that close call began in 1808. That was the year Charles Frémon turned up in Richmond, Virginia. The handsome newcomer claimed to be a fugitive from the French Revolution. He found work in Richmond as a teacher and painter. In 1810, Major John Pryor hired Frémon to teach French to his young wife, Anne.

The major was old enough to be Anne's grandfather. The loveless marriage had been arranged by Anne's family. Now she found comfort in Frémon's arms. In 1811, an outraged Pryor learned of the affair. He threatened to kill her. A day later, Anne and Frémon ran off. In those days, divorce was rare. Anne could live with Frémon, but she could not marry him.

The happy couple traveled widely. When their money ran out, they settled in Savannah, Georgia. Frémon taught dancing. Anne ran a boardinghouse. She gave birth to John Charles there. The most likely date was January 21, 1813. Anne later gave birth to a girl and a second son. Both died young.

Frémon's death in 1818 left Anne with a five-year-old child to support. Aided by friends, she settled in Charleston, South Carolina. The guests at her new boardinghouse knew her as Anne Frémont. Adding the "t" made the name seem more "American."

At age thirteen, young Frémont caught the eye of lawyer John Mitchell, who hired the boy as a clerk. When asked to survey a rice field, he impressed his boss with his skill and neatness. With the kindly lawyer paying the bills, Frémont enrolled at prep school. Within a year, he was reading Latin and Greek. In his spare time, he studied maps of the night skies.

In 1829, Frémont earned a scholarship to the College of Charleston. The sixteen-year-old was a clever student but a careless one. On sunny days, he cut class to explore Charleston's meadows and marshes. A schoolboy romance cost him more study time. Early in 1831, the college lost patience. With graduation only weeks away, Frémont was dismissed.

The young man soon found a new patron. Joel Poinsett is best known today for the poinsettia, the red Christmas flower he brought back from Mexico in the late 1820s. After he retired in the 1830s, the former ambassador took an interest in young Frémont. Noting the teenager's lack of maturity, Poinsett found him a job on the USS *Natchez*. Frémont's task was to teach math to the midshipmen. A voyage to South America kept him away from home until 1835.

Frémont grew up during the endless months at sea. When he returned, he had decided on a naval career. He switched goals after he was hired to be part of an army survey team. With two partners, Frémont spent the winter of 1836 mapping the Carolina woods. The trip gave him a crash course in wilderness survival. It also deepened his love of outdoor adventure.

Thanks to Poinsett, the U.S. Army commissioned Frémont as a second lieutenant. To his delight, he was

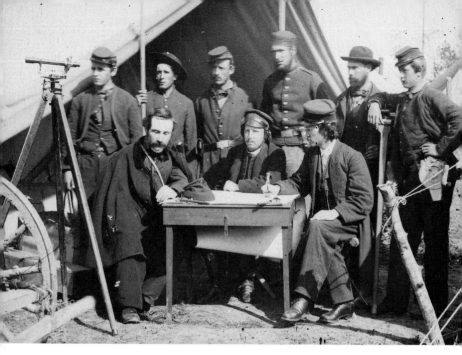

John Frémont joined the Corps of Topographical Engineers, a U.S. Army unit responsible for mapping out uncharted territories. In this Civil War photo, a team of topographical engineers are working at an army camp in Yorktown, Virginia.

assigned to the Corps of Topographical Engineers. In Washington, D.C., Frémont met Joseph Nicollet. The U.S. government had hired this famous explorer to map the lands beyond the Mississippi. Frémont jumped at Nicollet's offer to join his 1837 expedition.

The young officer quickly fell in love with the West. He hunted buffalo, made friends with fur traders, and survived a prairie fire. Back in Washington, Frémont drew detailed maps based on the party's survey work. He had found, as he later wrote, "the path which I was 'destined to walk.'"

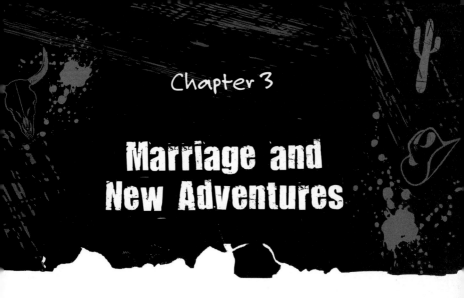

Chapter 3

Marriage and New Adventures

Two expeditions with Nicollet opened new doors for Frémont. One of his admirers was a senator from Missouri. Thomas Hart Benton was pushing the government to open the West to American settlers. He picked Frémont as the ideal man to explore the vast region. Frémont became a frequent guest at the Benton home.

In 1840, Frémont and fifteen-year-old Jessie Benton fell in love. The romance, however, alarmed Mrs. Benton, whose plans for Jessie did not include marriage to a poor army officer. For a time, the Bentons kept Frémont and Jessie apart. In October 1841, the lovers took matters into their own hands. They eloped.

The senator's anger soon cooled. The nation needed good maps of the West, and Nicollet was ill.

Thanks to Benton's influence, his son-in-law was given command of a new expedition. On May 2, 1842, Frémont left Washington. His goal was to find a route to South Pass in the Rocky Mountains.

From St. Louis, Frémont traveled up the Missouri by steamboat. It was on this trip that he met the great mountain man Kit Carson. Frémont hired Carson as his guide for $100 a month. The chance meeting led to a lifelong friendship.

The expedition left from Westport, Missouri, on June 10, 1842. Frémont's mule-drawn carts carried food, tools, a telescope, and a rubber boat. The men rolled out of their blankets at 4:30 each morning. After breakfast came the day's trek across miles of prairie. Frémont gathered specimens and filled his journals with detailed notes. At sunset, the men arranged the carts in a circle. Dinner was likely to be roast buffalo. Sentries stood watch, ready to repel a surprise attack.

Frémont split his party at a fork in the Platte River. Carson led one group north to Fort Laramie. Frémont took his group along the uncharted south fork. One of his jobs was to find sites for future forts. On July 9, he saw the Rockies for the first time. At Fort Laramie, an American Indian leader invited Frémont to a feast.

On his first western expedition in 1842, John Frémont met the famous scout, Kit Carson. Together, the two men helped open vast regions of the West to settlement. This photo of Carson (standing) and Frémont was taken in 1845.

As a guest, he could not refuse the steaming bowl of dog meat that his hosts had cooked for him.

A week later, Frémont turned west again. On August 8, the men reached South Pass (altitude 7,500 feet). By this time, Frémont was convinced that the trip had been too easy. To test himself, he climbed snowbound Gannet Peak (altitude 13,800 feet). When he reached the top, he planted an American flag there. On the return trip, Frémont lost his rubber boat and some of his journals in a descent through a series of river rapids.

By the end of October, the explorer was back in Washington. Two weeks later, Jessie gave birth to their first child, a daughter. They named her Elizabeth, but called her Lily. Frémont covered the infant with one of the flags he had flown in the Rockies. Over the next twelve years, the Frémonts had four more children— three boys and a girl. As often happened in those days, two died young.

Frémont turned to writing his report to Congress. To speed the task, he dictated much of it to Jessie. She polished his words as she wrote them down. When it was published, the 210-page report was widely read. Settlers used it as a trusted guide on their trek west.

In 1843, Frémont headed a second expedition. With Carson back to lead the way, the party explored the Great Salt Lake. In October, Frémont paddled a canoe down the mighty Columbia to Fort Vancouver. From Oregon, the party moved south. The route led into the great basin that lies between the Rockies and the Sierra Nevada.

Frémont hoped to find a fabled river that was supposed to flow to the Pacific Ocean. The river, he discovered, did not exist. No one could cross the mountains in winter, the local American Indians cautioned. The warnings did not stop Frémont. He pushed on toward California. Day after day, the party trudged through deep snow. Only Carson's skill as a guide made the crossing possible. In March 1844, the weary men reached safety in the Sacramento Valley.

Frémont chose a southern route for the return trip. On July 1, the party reached Bent's Fort on the Arkansas River. Five weeks later, Frémont stepped off a steamboat in St. Louis. For months, Jessie had feared that he was dead. Their reunion was a joyous one.

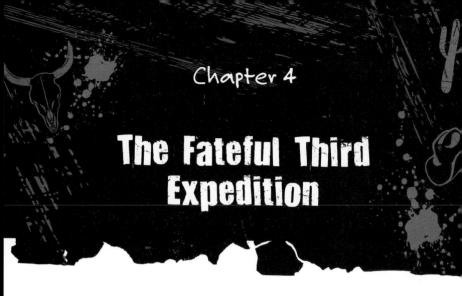

Chapter 4

The Fateful Third Expedition

ack in Washington, D.C., Frémont worked on his report. Jessie again served as his editor. Rushed into print early in 1845, the six-hundred-page report became a best-seller. The press hailed the thirty-two-year-old explorer as a national hero. Some called him "a Columbus of the Plains." Frémont preferred a simpler nickname: the Pathfinder.

Free at last of its ties to Mexico, Texas joined the Union in 1845. At the same time, Frémont's reports were fueling the nation's thirst for westward expansion. President James K. Polk and Senator Benton met with Frémont to plan a third expedition.

The expedition's stated task was to explore the region between the Arkansas and Red rivers. Frémont, however, had a grander idea. As he later wrote: "I saw the way opening . . . [to] make the Pacific Ocean the western boundary of the United States."

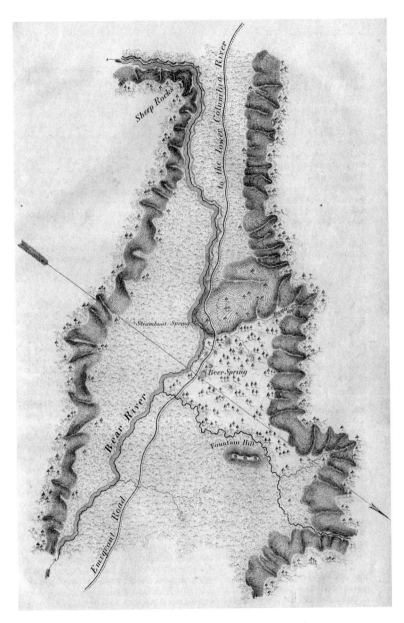

Frémont illustrated his reports with detailed maps of the western territories. This 1845 map spotlights Wyoming's Emigrant Road where it runs parallel to the Bear River.

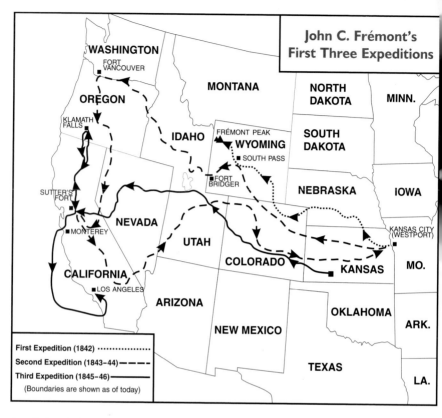

John C. Frémont's
First Three Expeditions

First Expedition (1842) ············
Second Expedition (1843–44) —————
Third Expedition (1845–46) ————
(Boundaries are shown as of today)

John Frémont's objective for his third expedition was to set the Pacific Ocean as the western boundary of the United States. Frémont's success on his first three expeditions into uncharted territory tested everyone's skill, courage, and endurance. This map traces the routes of the Pathfinder's first three journeys.

By August, the expedition had reached Bent's Fort in southeastern Colorado. Carson left his ranch and joined his friend there. Frémont sent half of his men to carry out the Red River survey. By November, the rest of Frémont's party had reached western Nevada. Carson led the way along the Truckee River. Soon they were climbing into the Sierra Nevada.

Winter snows had not yet clogged the passes. Frémont reached Sutter's Fort on December 9. After five days of feasting, the Americans rode south. They set up a secret camp in the San Joaquin Valley.

With eight mountain men as backup, Frémont rode to Monterey. Thomas Larkin, the U.S. consul, took him to the military governor. The visit did not please Governor José Castro, who knew his rich province was in danger. American settlers came in a steady stream. British warships lay offshore. Castro feared their captains would try to claim California for Queen Victoria.

Frémont told Castro he was there to conduct a survey. Castro did not believe him. He feared that the visitors would try to conquer California. When the mountain men insulted some local women, he asked Frémont to leave. The Pathfinder snarled that the order was an even bigger insult. He built a crude log fort and raised the American flag.

On March 9, 1846, Frémont left the fort and headed north. His party reached Klamath Falls late in April. On the night of May 8, Klamath warriors attacked the camp. Three of Frémont's men died in the bloody battle. He avenged their deaths by burning a Klamath fishing village.

A courier arrived that same day with secret orders that made Frémont's mission quite clear. War with Mexico was coming; California must be held for the United States. In January 1847, after six months of fierce attacks and counterattacks, the Mexicans surrendered. On January 16, Commodore Robert Stockton picked Frémont to be governor. On the same day, General Stephen Kearny ordered Frémont to take no action without his approval. To obey Kearny was to disobey Stockton. In the midst of victory, Frémont found himself in serious trouble.

Frémont sent Kearny a letter. He would obey Stockton, he wrote, until the dispute was settled. Kearny backed off. Pushing too hard, he realized, might start a civil war. He peppered Frémont with orders but let him stay on as governor.

The Pathfinder did his best to govern the territory. He won the trust of the Californios by treating them fairly. He also signed purchase orders that ran up a $60,000 debt. In March, orders arrived that confirmed Kearny as governor. Frémont's brief term came to a sudden end. On March 22, Frémont agreed to accept Kearny's authority. That small triumph was not enough for the general. He could not touch Stockton, but Colonel Frémont was his to command.

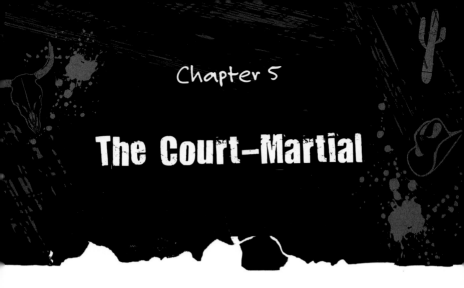

Chapter 5

The Court-Martial

In May 1847, General Kearny ordered Frémont to march east with him. When the column pulled out, Kearny rode at its head. Frémont was left to bring up the rear. At Kearny's orders, he left his survey equipment behind. By now, the entire country knew about the clash between the two men. One rumor said that Kearny planned to have Frémont shot.

The march ended at Fort Leavenworth, Kansas. Kearny had not forgiven the junior officer's refusal to obey orders. On August 22, he placed Frémont under arrest. The charges were mutiny, failure to obey orders, and bad conduct. Frémont's fate would be decided by a court-martial. A guilty verdict could mean a death sentence. Bound by orders to report to Washington for trial, Frémont headed east. At each stop, crowds gathered to cheer him. Jessie was waiting at a steamboat landing on the Missouri River. Together, the Frémonts went on to St. Louis. As Jessie wrote: "We lived alone . . . on a happy island surrounded by a sea of troubles."

In Washington, Frémont learned that his mother was ill. She died in South Carolina hours before he could reach her side. When Frémont returned to Washington, Senator Benton joined his team of lawyers. Frémont spoke in his own defense, however. Benton could advise him, but only an army officer could address the court.

Jessie saw that his troubles had aged her husband. He was only thirty-four, but his dark hair was streaked with gray. Some of the joy had gone out of his gray-blue eyes. A slender five feet nine inches tall, he looked every inch the stern soldier-explorer.

The trial opened on November 2. Thirteen regular army officers served as judge and jury. Eleven of them had been in the army for thirty years or more. These old veterans did not favor young heroes. Some resented the help Frémont had received from his powerful father-in-law.

Frémont spoke at length. He drove home the point that he was the victim of a power struggle. Kearny was punishing him, he said, but Stockton was the real target. When called to the stand, Kearny proved to be a poor witness. He stated a fact one day, then denied it the next. At one point, the general said that Frémont had come to him to ask to be made governor. However, Frémont produced Kearny's note of June 17, 1846. It said, "I wish to see you on business." Clearly, it was Kearny who had asked for the meeting. The general's memory could not be trusted.

John Frémont returned to Washington, D.C., for his court-martial, which began on November 2, 1847. Although he was only thirty-four years old, the rigorous life of an explorer and soldier had aged the Pathfinder. He posed for this portrait in 1856.

Next, Frémont zeroed in on the delayed arrest. His angry letter to Kearny was dated January 17, 1847. Why had Kearny waited until August to arrest him? Frémont told the court, "Public duty ought to have induced him to warn [Stockton] of my [dangerous] conduct."

Frémont had counted on Stockton's testimony. Instead, his former commander turned out to be a vague and rambling witness. In California, Stockton had stood up to Kearny. Now he claimed that his orders had been unclear. He said he had lacked the power to appoint Frémont to the office of governor. In private, Frémont accused Stockton of making a secret deal with Kearny.

Late in January 1848, the court announced its verdict. Frémont was found "guilty on all charges." Instead of a firing squad, his sentence called for dismissal from the army. Six of the officers entered a plea for clemency. Frémont, they noted, had been caught in the middle of the Kearny-Stockton conflict. He was guilty—but it was not his fault.

President Polk threw out the charge of mutiny. Then, to safeguard army discipline, he found Frémont guilty of the other charges. To soften the blow, Polk offered a pardon. If Frémont took the pardon, he could stay in the army.

Frémont turned down Polk's offer. He had done nothing, he said, "to merit the finding of the court." The verdict, he argued, was a stain on his honor. He quit the army and turned his face westward.

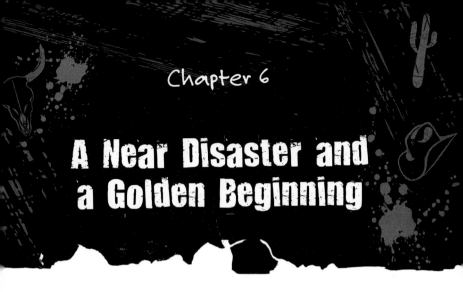

Chapter 6

A Near Disaster and a Golden Beginning

Senator Benton helped line up backers for a fourth expedition. Frémont's new mission was to survey a railroad route from St. Louis to California. Tragedy struck while the Frémonts were traveling up the Missouri River. Two days before they reached Westport (today's Kansas City), their sickly one-year-old son, Benton, died. Jessie blamed the stress of the court-martial for the baby's death.

The Frémonts said good-bye at Westport. They planned to meet in California. Jessie turned eastward. Her sea voyage via Panama was the easier route, but still it was a long, difficult journey. Frémont trekked westward. He was sure he would find a route across the Rockies that could be used all through the year.

The mountain men at Bent's Fort told Frémont he was crazy. Snow was already falling in Colorado's San Juan Mountains. Frémont was not alarmed. He boasted that he would be in California in thirty-five days. This time, Kit Carson was not there to guide him. Frémont hired "Old Bill" Williams to lead the way.

The party bought its last supplies at a tiny Colorado town called Hardscrabble. Ahead lay high peaks, fifty-foot snowdrifts, and howling blizzards. The temperature dropped as the men slogged forward. On December 6, Richard Kern wrote: "We all looked like old Time or Winter—icicles an inch long were pendant from our moustache & beard."

On some days, the men were hard pressed to claw their way half a mile. Feed for the pack animals ran out. The horses and mules chewed on their leather harnesess. Half of them died. Frémont suffered from the headaches and nausea of altitude sickness.

Williams could not find the pass. With food running low, the men ate the dead mules. To keep from freezing, they slept in snow caves. Frostbite and snow blindness were common complaints. Despite the hardships, Frémont refused to turn back. Later, when reports of the expedition reached the public, his admirers called him a brave trailblazer. His critics said he was a stubborn fool.

Some of the men lay down, too weak to go on. Frémont sent four of the stronger men to bring help

In this campaign ad, John Frémont is shown planting an American flag at the top of a mountain peak. Unfortunately, his fourth expedition did not provide a similar triumph. Frémont's trek over Colorado's San Juan Mountains would have been difficult in any season. In winter, storms made the trek nearly impossible.

from Taos, 160 miles away. Then he led the others down the mountain. When the rescue party did not return, Frémont set out with a second group. Six days later, he caught up with the first party. One man was dead; the others were starving. On January 21, limping on a frost-bitten foot, Frémont stumbled into Taos. Kit Carson put him to bed and fed him hot soup. Then Carson rode out to rescue the survivors.

Frémont gave up his survey and rode on to California. Along the trail, he met a caravan bursting with news. Gold had been found at Sutter's Fort! Frémont had planned to sell the forty thousand acres he had purchased at Mariposa. Now he realized that he owned a big chunk of the gold country. On the spot, he struck a deal with a group of these early forty-niners. Prospect my land, he told them, and we'll split any gold you find.

Jessie reached San Francisco in June 1849. Frémont joined her there. It was not long before his miners struck it rich at Mariposa. The Frémonts' cupboards

In these 1860 illustrations published in *Harper's Monthly*, the Frémont Mill and gold field in Mariposa, California, are shown at left. At right, gold prospectors work a claim. Frémont struck a deal with the early forty-niners when gold was discovered in California. In exchange for prospecting his land at Mariposa, Frémont promised to share any gold the miners found.

were soon filled with sacks of gold ore. Jessie guessed that each sack was worth $25,000. Those rich gold-fields, however, had never been surveyed. Frémont did not know the exact boundaries of his claims. Claim jumpers moved in to prospect for gold on his land.

Despite the problem with land titles, the Frémonts were happy. Jessie furnished their ranch house with fine furniture shipped from the East. As California moved toward statehood, the Pathfinder took on a new role. The legislature picked him to represent the new state as one of its U.S. senators.

Frémont took his seat in Congress on September 10, 1850. In the twenty-one days before the session ended, he introduced eighteen bills. Back in California, he paid a price for holding strong antislavery views. In 1851, the pro-slavery legislature replaced him.

The ex-senator had little time to regret the loss of his seat. Town building was taking up much of his time. Mariposa was growing fast—and Frémont owned the land on which the town stood.

Chapter 7

The Pathfinder Runs for President

In 1852, Jessie and John Charles Frémont made their first trip to Europe. In London, the Royal Geographical Society gave the Pathfinder a gold medal. Frémont also found time to sell stock in his mines to British investors. By September, he was back at Westport Landing. For the fifth and final time, he led an expedition westward. This time, he found a pass through the San Juan Mountains.

With his survey work done, Frémont returned to politics. Kansas and Nebraska were ready to become states. Would they be slave or free? The Compromise of 1820 had kept slavery south of the east-west map line of 36°30'. Because Kansas and Nebraska lay north of that line, they would be free states. In 1854, however, Congress passed a new law. All new states could choose to be either free or slave. Kansas and

Nebraska now could enter the Union as slave states. Many abolitionists (people who opposed slavery) felt betrayed by this act. They joined forces with other groups to form the new Republican Party.

The shadow of slavery hung over the coming election. Slave owners wanted their own man in the White House. In 1855, some leading Democrats offered to back Frémont for president. There was a condition attached to the offer, however. Frémont would have to support all laws that protected slavery. The chance to run for the nation's highest office was tempting. After a long talk with Jessie, Frémont turned down the offer. He would not change his belief that slavery was wrong.

Early in 1856, a second group approached him. The Republicans needed a strong antislavery candidate. If he was a national hero, so much the better. In June, the Republican convention chose Frémont to be the party's first presidential candidate.

Frémont faced a three-way race. The Democrats bypassed President Franklin Pierce. A former senator from Pennsylvania named James Buchanan took his place. Millard Fillmore, a former president, ran on the American Party ticket. That party was better known as the Know-Nothings. The nickname grew out of its

Col. JOHN C. FREMONT,
REPUBLICAN CANDIDATE FOR PRESIDENT OF THE UNITED STATES.

An 1856 campaign poster urges voters to elect Republican presidential candidate John C. Frémont. The party ran a strong campaign, but the Pathfinder lost the election by a slim margin.

birth as a secret club. When asked about their party, members answered, "I know nothing."

The Republicans ran a strong campaign. Torchlight parades snaked through the nation's streets. Crowds chanted, "Free men, free speech, free soil, and Frémont!" FRÉMONT AND VICTORY banners flapped in the breeze. Books about the Pathfinder hit the newsstands. Color posters sold for a dollar. An Illinois lawyer named Abraham Lincoln made more than ninety speeches for Frémont.

The forty-three-year-old candidate needed support. He could not make small talk. He had almost no sense of humor. In an age of orators, he was a weak public speaker. Most of all, he hated the chore of shaking hands at county fairs. He said he felt like a prize horse on display.

As Jessie described it, the campaign was "a trial by mud." Frémont, who rarely touched liquor, was called a drunkard. Democrats dug up the old story that his parents had not been married. The Know-Nothing Party, which hated Catholics, shrieked that Frémont was a secret Catholic. After all, its leaders pointed out, his father had been a Catholic. And hadn't the Frémonts been married by a priest? Urged to answer the charges, Frémont held his tongue. He relied on friends to say that he was a Protestant. Even his role in the struggle for California was questioned. He was called a phony hero and a land-grabber.

The South threatened to leave the Union if Frémont won. Fear that the country might be split helped Buchanan win 174 electoral votes to Frémont's 114. The loss of Pennsylvania and Illinois made the difference. If he had won those two states, Frémont would have been elected the fifteenth president.

Fourteen-year-old Lily Frémont was more upset than her father. The teenager had looked forward to "four delightful years" in the White House.

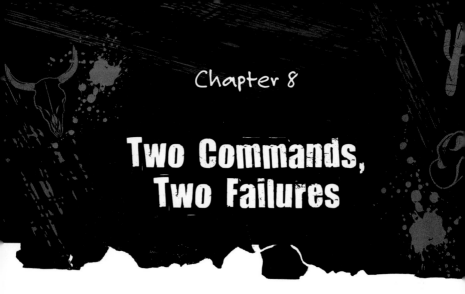

Chapter 8

Two Commands, Two Failures

With Jessie's father ailing, the Frémonts stayed in Washington. After Senator Benton died in April 1858, the family moved back to California. Frémont still had problems with claim jumpers, but the mines were producing well. To please Jessie, he built a home on San Francisco Bay. She loved the view across the Golden Gate.

The election of 1860 sent shock waves through the South. With Abraham Lincoln in the White House, slavery seemed doomed. By February 1861, seven southern states had withdrawn from the Union. Frémont was in France when the first shots of the Civil War were fired in April. Acting on his own, he bought ten thousand rifles for the Union army. Then he sailed home to volunteer.

President Lincoln's top general was the aging Winfield Scott. The president picked Frémont as one of Scott's field commanders. The new major general took command of the Department of the West. This vast region stretched from the Mississippi River to the Rockies. Even though Missouri was a slave state, Lincoln hoped to keep it in the Union. To do so, Frémont would have to be both general and diplomat. He failed at both tasks.

Frémont arrived in St. Louis on July 25, 1861. Once he had led a few hundred men. Now he gave orders to thirty thousand troops. Most were poorly trained and badly equipped. In the first of many mistakes, he filled his staff with volunteer officers from Europe. Many proved to be useless. Working night and day, Frémont drew up a grand plan to advance down the Mississippi River. If he had been successful, the move would have split the South.

Southern troops spoiled the plan by mauling Union forces in southwest Missouri. Frémont saw that he was outgunned. He bombarded Washington with demands for more troops, guns, and supplies, to no avail. The war in the east was eating up the lion's share of the North's military resources. With unrest spreading across Missouri, Frémont declared martial law on

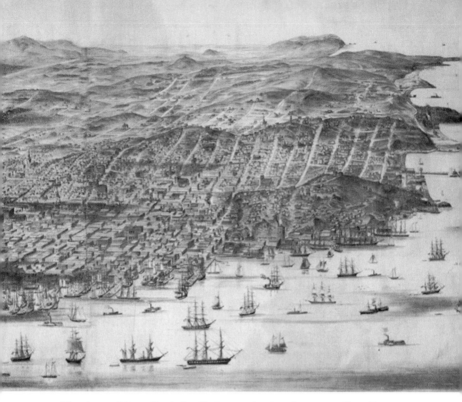

To please his wife, John Frémont built a home in San Francisco that gave Jessie a view across the Golden Gate. This drawing captures a bird's-eye view of San Francisco Bay in 1864.

August 30. The action gave him the right to hang captured guerrillas. It also freed the state's slaves.

The news brought cheers from abolitionists. President Lincoln did not join the applause. He feared that Frémont's rash acts would hurt the Union cause. Kentucky, a slave state like Missouri, could easily be pushed into rebellion. As gently as he could, Lincoln asked Frémont to cancel his orders. Frémont responded by sending Jessie to argue his case. Lincoln replied by giving Frémont a direct order. The slaves were not to be freed. No one would be hanged. When the dispute became public, Lincoln had to prove he was in control. He ordered Frémont's removal. The Pathfinder's command had lasted only a few short months.

Some key Republicans argued that their hero deserved a second chance. In March 1862, Lincoln put Frémont in command of the Mountain Department. From the start, his problems multiplied. He was told to attack Knoxville, Tennessee, after marching his troops south from West Virginia. The route crossed 250 miles of rain-soaked woodlands. The 25,000 troops had to live off the land.

The plan soon bogged down. Short rations and long marches left the soldiers hungry and tired. Some of them were forced to go barefoot. By contrast, Stonewall Jackson's rebel troops were fit and rested. Frémont did his best, but he could not trap his clever foe. When Jackson did stop to fight, he won five battles in a row.

Lincoln sent General Carl Schurz to investigate. Schurz's report cleared Frémont of blame. "The government has plenty of provisions," he wrote, "and our soldiers die of hunger." Lincoln then organized his scattered forces into the Army of the Potomac. Frémont was given a corps command under General John Pope.

In March 1862, Frémont was ordered to lead 25,000 troops on a strenuous march from West Virginia to attack Knoxville, Tennessee. This illustration shows Frémont's weary, ill-fed soldiers as they marched through the Shenandoah Valley in pursuit of Confederate general, Thomas "Stonewall" Jackson.

Frémont's pride would not allow him to take orders from the younger man. Lincoln let him resign his corps command in June 1862. Frémont spent the next year waiting for orders that never came. On August 12, 1863, he resigned from the army. Even if the Union did not need him, his mines did.

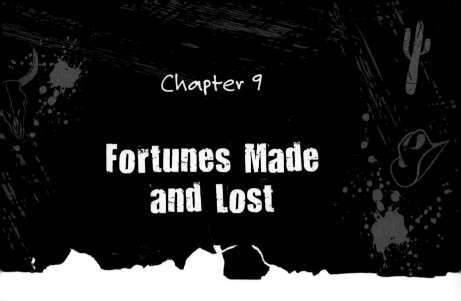

Chapter 9

Fortunes Made and Lost

O ut of the army and free of politics, Frémont turned to business. For a time, he lived a rich man's life in New York City. Servants staffed a fine brownstone at 21 West Nineteenth Street. In the summer, the family relaxed on an estate near Tarrytown.

The good times did not last. Frémont's mines now produced more debts than gold. He was forced to sell the Mariposa estate in 1863. But that was not the only bad news. The army took his land beside the Golden Gate to build a fort. The Frémonts were never paid for the loss.

Radical Republicans felt the war was dragging on too long. In 1864, they asked Frémont to run for president against Lincoln. The Pathfinder turned them down. He knew that changing leaders during wartime would harm the country.

Frémont's new passion was to build a railroad to the West Coast. His first scheme fell apart in 1867. Unable to pay his mounting debts, he lost his railroad holdings in Missouri. Frémont bounced back, gaining control of the Memphis, El Paso, and Pacific Railroad. Texas attempted to speed construction by granting 18 million acres to the railroad. European brokers raised $10 million by selling railroad bonds. In France, brokers made false claims. To woo investors, they said that the bonds were backed by the U.S. government. When the truth came out three years later, the French government accused Frémont of fraud.

The best route lay across federal land in New Mexico and Arizona. Frémont asked Congress for the right to build the railroad across this territory. The government turned down his request. That defeat, combined with legal problems in Europe, doomed the project. In 1872, he was forced to sell his New York homes. "General," his lawyer said, "if you keep trusting people . . . they will ruin you."

For a time, Jessie earned money by writing magazine articles and children's books. Although the Frémonts lacked money, they did not lack friends. In 1878, some supporters talked Congress into appointing Frémont to the post of governor of Arizona Territory.

The $2,600-a-year salary did not go far in remote Prescott. A four-room wooden house rented for $90 a month. Hiring a cook cost another $40. Frémont traveled widely, dreaming up grand schemes for making the desert bloom. He was happy, but Jessie's heart could not stand the strain of

Tiring after years of hard work, seventy-three-year-old John Frémont began writing his memoirs in 1886. This photo of the aging Pathfinder was taken in 1890.

the mile-high altitude. She moved back to a cottage on Staten Island, New York. Frémont resigned in 1881 and joined her.

In 1886, the seventy-three-year-old Frémont settled down to write his memoirs. Once again, Jessie served as his editor. The first volume ended with the story of his third expedition. Frémont had high hopes for the book, but it sold poorly. The publisher did not ask for a second volume.

The Frémonts retired to a quiet life in Los Angeles. In 1890, Congress gave Frémont back his old army rank and a pension of $6,000 a year. The aging

Pathfinder did not have long to enjoy the money. He fell ill while on a visit to New York that same year. His appendix burst, and he died on July 13. He was buried near Tarrytown.

Jessie could not afford to travel east to the funeral. On hearing of her plight, a woman's club gave her a cottage in Los Angeles. Later, Congress awarded Jessie a pension of $2,000 a year. She lived quietly with her memories until her death in 1902.

Was John Charles Frémont the great hero Jessie said he was? Some critics say he walked in the footsteps of earlier explorers. Others point to his failures as a Civil War general and as a businessman. Perhaps the critics should look at the map. All through the West, people have named streets, towns, and counties for Frémont. California takes pride in its General Frémont Grove of giant sequoias. There is a Frémont Peak in Wyoming and a Frémont Pass in Colorado.

Perhaps railroad builder Colin Huntington said it best. He once told Frémont, "You forget, General, our railroad goes over your buried campfires."

Glossary

abolitionist—Someone who worked to abolish slavery in the years before the Civil War.

altitude sickness—An illness marked by headache, stomach upset, and fatigue. It is brought on by living and working high above sea level.

annex—To add territory to a state or country.

brownstone—A multi-storied home built of or faced with a brown-colored sandstone.

Californios—Wealthy landowners who dominated California in the years before the United States won control of the province from Mexico.

claim jumper—A miner who prospects for minerals on land that belongs to someone else.

clemency—The act of a president or a state governor that cancels a court-imposed punishment.

commission—A government document that appoints someone to a particular rank or office.

court-martial—A court that tries officers and enlisted personnel who have been accused of crimes under military law.

duel—An armed combat between two people, usually fought under strict rules.

electoral vote—Under the U.S. Constitution, voters in each state choose a group of electors who cast the electoral votes that elect the president and vice president.

elope—To run away to be married.

guerrilla—A member of a small, fast-moving group of raiders who operate outside the normal laws of warfare.

legislature—A group of lawmakers elected by the voters of a state or nation.

martial law—Temporary rule of a civilian population by military authorities.

memoirs—An author's account of his or her personal experiences; an autobiography.

militia—Part-time soldiers who are called to duty in times of emergency.

mountain man—One of the fiercely independent hunters, explorers, and trappers who roamed the western mountain wilderness.

mutiny—Open rebellion by members of the armed forces against their commander.

pardon—The act by which a president or a governor grants legal forgiveness for a crime.

pension—Monthly payments made to ex-soldiers and other retired workers.

staff officer—A lower-ranking military officer who has the job of advising a commanding officer.

Further Reading

Books

Calvert, Patricia. *Kit Carson: He Led the Way.* New York: Marshall Cavendish Benchmark, 2007.

Faber, Harold. *John Charles Frémont: Pathfinder to the West.* New York: Benchmark Books, 2003.

Hossell, Karen Price. *John C. Frémont.* Chicago: Heinemann Library, 2003.

Souza, D. M. *John C. Frémont.* New York: Franklin Watts, 2004.

Witteman, Barbara. *John Charles Frémont: Western Pathfinder.* Mankato, Minn.: Bridgestone Books, 2003.

Internet Addresses

Captain John Charles Frémont and the Bear Flag Revolt
<http://www.militarymuseum.org/fremont.html>

John Charles Frémont
<http://www.civilwarstlouis.com/bios/fremont.htm>

PBS—New Perspectives on the West: Events in the West, 1840–1850
<http://www.pbs.org/weta/thewest/events/1840_1850.htm>

Index

A
abolitionists, 33, 38
American Indians, 14–16, 21

B
Benton, Thomas Hart, 9, 13, 18, 24, 27, 36
Buchanan, James, 33, 35

C
California, 5–8, 21–22, 27, 28, 31, 36–40, 44
Californios, 8, 22
Carson, Kit, 14, 17, 20, 28, 29
Castro, José, 6, 7, 21
Civil War, 36–40

D
dueling, 9

F
Fillmore, Millard, 33
Frémon, Charles, 9–10
Frémont (Pryor), Anne, 9–10, 24
Frémont, Jessie Benton, 13, 16, 18, 23–24, 27, 30–31, 35, 36, 38, 39, 42–44
Frémont, John C.
 antislavery views of, 31, 33
 army career, 11–12, 23–26, 36–40
 as author, 16, 18, 43
 birth, childhood/family life, 9–12
 California role, 5–8, 21–22, 36–40
 children, 16, 27
 court-martial of, 23–26
 death, 43–44
 as explorer, 13–21, 27–29
 as governor, 22, 42–43
 marriage, 13
 Presidential campaign, 32–35
 as U.S. senator, 31

G
Gannet Peak, 16
gold mining, 30–32, 36, 41
Great Salt Lake expedition, 17

J
Jackson, Andrew, 9
Jackson, Thomas "Stonewall," 39

K
Kearny, Stephen, 8, 22–26
Know-Nothings, 33–35

L
Larkin, Thomas, 21
Lincoln, Abraham, 34, 36, 37, 38–39
Los Osos, 5–6

N
Nicollet, Joseph, 12, 13

P
Poinsett, Joel, 11
Polk, James K., 18, 26
Pryor, John, 9–10

R
railroad building, 42
Red River survey, 18–21

S
San Juan Mountains expeditions, 27–29, 32
Schurz, Carl, 39
Scott, Winfield, 37
slavery, 31–33, 36, 37–39
Sloat, John, 6
South Pass expedition, 14–16
Stockton, Robert, 6–7, 22, 24–26

T
Texas, 5, 18

W
Williams, "Old Bill," 28